HOW TO FIX BROKE

The Personal Finance System for Working Families

by:

Milton B Freeman, Jr
Certified Financial Education Instructor

About the Author

Milton B. Freeman, Jr. is the owner of EFI Financial Education Services, LLC in Atlanta, GA. As a Certified Financial Education Instructor (CFEI), he partners with government entities and private sector organizations to deliver financial education workshops, seminars, and training to both adult citizens and students. In the community, he serves as a licensed insurance producer, personal finance coach, and notary public. Financial experiences in his life motivated Milton to introduce his children (now teenagers) to financial literacy, fiscal responsibility, and entrepreneurship before they were old enough to work jobs. The foundation of those teachings are outlined in the writing of his first published work, *"How to Fix Broke: The Personal Finance Plan for Working Families"*. Milton's message to anyone he serves is, *"Exercise Financial Intelligence"*.

ACKNOWLEDGEMENTS

Interactions with my father front-loaded me with the necessary amount of knowledge, courage, and general wherewithal to make my way through life after his untimely departure. My mom helps ensure that my spiritual foundation stays firm. A special "thank you" is extended to my sister for her trust and loyalty through tumultuous times of the past.

I am appreciative of the love and respect that I am shown in my household. In my wife, I have found a virtuous woman, whose "price is far above rubies". My children make me proud, and have made the price worth paying to be called, "Daddy". Thank you, family.

DEDICATION

This book is dedicated to my grandparents (my lineage), a generation of people born during "The Great Depression", who despite the racial hostility and socioeconomic imbalances for blacks in the Jim Crow south persevered and created in their homes, environments of security and stability for multiple generations of offspring.

I appreciate my grandfathers, men of military service who were deemed less than worthy of respect from the "home country" upon their respective returns from fighting in foreign lands. They accomplished more with less while painting clear pictures of manhood and household leadership for my father and uncles to observe and pass down to my generation of men.

I am eternally grateful for my grandmothers, who were not only skilled women; but were dedicated, affectionate, and efficient keepers of their tribes. Their displays of womanhood and lady-like elegance were instilled in my mother and aunts to be passed down to my generation of siblings and first cousins.

The names,
Mr. Charlie R. & Edith Freeman and **Mr. Lacy T. & Emory Harris** may continue to go unmentioned in books alongside the great names of history; so, I give honor where honor is due to the ones whose sacrifices paved the way for me to have the power in my hands to publish their names in my work.

Contents

INTRODUCTION 8

STEP 1: FINANCIAL THERAPY 11

   How Beliefs Create and Limit Your Financial Reality 15

   Negative Money Beliefs 16

   Positive Money Beliefs 20

   Positive Money Beliefs in Action 23

   Step 1: Action Exercise #1 Goal Setting 24

   Step 1: Action Exercise #2 Goal Setting Actions 26

STEP 2: MAKE MONEY 28

   Step 2 Exercise: Personal Earning Exploration 32

STEP 3: PAY YOURSELF FIRST 34

   Pay Yourself First: How to Do It and Why 35

STEP 4: TAKE CONTROL OF YOUR FINANCES 39

   Week 1: Create a Budget 40

   Week 2: Establish a Savings Plan 43

   Week 3: Plan to Eliminate Debt 47

   Week 4: Increase Income 52

   10 Ideas for Boosting Your Income 54

Take Control of Your Finances: Checklist 57

STEP 5: PUT YOUR MONEY TO WORK 59

    Why Should I Invest? 61

    Am I Ready to Invest? 62

    How Can I Start Investing? 63

    ETFs/Index Funds/REITS/Mutual Funds 67

    Cryptocurrency 71

    Common Myths About Cryptocurrencies 73

    9 Golden Rules of Investing 77

STEP 6: GET INSURED 80

    Life Insurance 81

    Health Insurance 91

    Long-Term Disability Insurance 95

    Homeowner's Insurance 98

    Automobile Insurance 99

STEP 7: BOOST YOUR SKILLS 100

    Increase Your Earning Potential Without Loans 100

CONCLUSION 111

RESOURCES 114

ALL RIGHTS RESERVED. No part of this report may be modified or altered in any form whatsoever, electronic, or mechanical, including photocopying, recording, or by any informational storage or retrieval system without express written, dated, and signed permission from the author.

AFFILIATE DISCLAIMER. The short, direct, non-legal version is this: Some of the links in this report may be affiliate links which means that I earn money if you choose to buy from that vendor at some point in the near future. I do not choose which products and services to promote based upon which pay me the most, I choose based upon my decision of which I would recommend to a dear friend. You will never pay more for an item by clicking through my affiliate link, and, may pay less since I negotiate special offers for my readers that are not available elsewhere.

DISCLAIMER AND/OR LEGAL NOTICES: The information presented herein represents the view of the author as of the date of publication. Because of the rate with which conditions change, the author reserves the right to alter and update his opinion based on the new conditions. The report is for informational purposes only. While every attempt has been made to verify the information provided in this report, neither the author nor his affiliates/partners assume any responsibility for errors, inaccuracies, or omissions. Any slights of people or organizations are unintentional. If advice concerning legal or related matters is needed, the services of a fully qualified professional should be sought. This report is not intended for use as a source of legal or accounting advice. You should be aware of any laws which govern business transactions or other business practices in your country and state. Any reference to any person or business whether living or dead is purely coincidental.

Copyright © EFI FINANCIAL EDUCATION SERVICES, LLC 2021
Cover Design: Thornton Online Marketing
Paperback: ISBN: 978-1-7374637-5-7

INTRODUCTION

I want to congratulate you for operating in the ***Preparation Stage of Behavior Change***, which is demonstrated by your reading of this book.

Understand that you have passed through the ***Pre-Contemplation Stage of Behavior Change***, where you were in denial or simply failed to realize that your financial behavior needed to be addressed. Recall being awarded your first credit card. For some, all that mattered was, "I don't have to pay today!" ...not knowing or not caring that payments have to be made on time. The financial conditions one lives under today are indeed the reaping of seeds sown several years ago.

Whether it was a need, maturation, or a simple reality check, you moved through the ***Contemplation Stage of Behavior Change***. This means that you had a growing concern about handling your money and doing some things differently. Perhaps you've been through the pain of not qualifying for a car loan or experiencing the hurt of not being approved for a place to live. Whatever the case may be, past financial behaviors have affected or are affecting your "right now" needs.

As previously mentioned, this reader of this book is met at the ***Preparation Stage of Behavior Change***. You have overcome procrastination and "what ifs" about addressing your financial behavior. You have decided that now is the time. As we move through the chapters of this book, you will list goals, increase your morale, become motivated, and progressively transition into the ***Action Stage of Behavior Change***. This is where you will form financial habits, develop financial strategies, and implement personal systems that will guide you in executing a financial game plan.

Envision yourself operating in the *Maintenance Stage of Behavior Change*, spending with purpose; and strategizing with intent to build and grow financially. This step is where changes in behavior and productive habits are a new way of life. Think about the example that you can set for your children, and the enriching conversations you can have in the car or at dinner.

In this stage, unfortunately, exists the possibility of a relapse into reverting to past behaviors. This can come due to overconfidence driven by your successes or disappointments driven by failures (things not going according to plan). With mental fortitude and a track record of accomplishments, you should not allow yourself to be swallowed up by a relapse, resulting in you going back to detrimental financial behaviors of the past (overspending, bank overdrafts, late payments).

I believe that you will transcend relapsing and operate over the long run in the **Termination Stage of Behavior Change**. This is where positive behavior changes are in place, and you have moved beyond any temptation to revert to negative and costly money management behavior.

I have experienced the emotional roller coaster of a financial transformation. It was more specifically, in my case, a financial recovery. Bouncing back from a difficult time financially is what makes me bold enough to pen this book, conduct financial literacy workshops, and facilitate one-on-one financial coaching sessions. Earning the status of Certified Financial Education Instructor came in 2018. Part of that program introduced me to the stages of behavior mentioned above:
The Transtheoretical Model of Behavior Change.

A change in financial mindset, behavior, and/or an increase in income must occur if you want to enhance the trajectory of your financial future.

If you know that you should be achieving great things, but just can't quite seem to get there, I sincerely say that no situation is 100% hopeless. The first step towards taking control is just a decision away.

As you move through this book, you will learn how to nurture your mindset about money and establish a position of control in your life. You will blow up many of the money myths that have possibly shaped your financial way of thinking. Additionally, you will build a financial game plan that will help you get the most out of the money you earn. You will find the motivation to monetize the talents and skills you possess. Ultimately, you will be able to engage your school-age and young adult children or grandchildren with a mindset of financial intelligence, making financial literacy part of your legacy.

STEP 1: FINANCIAL THERAPY

Fix Your Money Beliefs and Change your Life

The reality of needing to change my money beliefs hit me in January 1996. I was 21 years old. My spirits were almost broken by having to get dressed for another fourteen-hour day of working on an outdoor loading dock in twenty-degree weather, intensified by a wind chill factor of -5. Fourteen months earlier, almost overnight, I had gone from being a dependent college student to being the protector and provider of the household due to the unexpected passing of my father.

It was a rough and hurtful time for me. My #1 guy was gone, and the matter of seeing about my family was not a drill. It was no more of the "when you get out into the real world…" stuff that people say all while you're growing up. With the welfare of mom and sister at the top of my list of priorities, I had taken a job that paid well enough to do what I needed to do. But while putting on long johns and layering up that day in January '96, I felt low. Not because I had to go to work; but because I knew that I was giving in to the thought of having to do that job for 30 years or until retirement.

I felt like I was in a game of Spades, holding a hand of only clubs and hearts. No Aces. No Kings. No Jokers. A beautiful sunny day with blue skies and a day of pouring rain were both the same to me. I couldn't tell a difference between the two, and there was no light at the end of my tunnel. Fortunately, I had the attitude of making that Queen of Clubs bring me a book. Spades players understand!

I didn't fold completely but ended up putting in a lot of back-bending work hours. That was the only way I could see to make the money I needed at the time.

The Power of Beliefs

Are you aware that changing your financial life isn't so much about changing the way you work as much as it is changing the way you think? And do you realize that negative or false money beliefs will not only stunt your economic growth; but will be passed down generationally if the cycle goes unbroken?

Would you find it crazy if you were told that the limits of your earning potential were tied to the limits of your beliefs? Your faith, even?

For many of our lives, the popular belief has been that the only way to have more money or to "make it" is to either:

1. Win the lottery
2. Work harder (overtime; second jobs; even 3rd jobs)

The odds of winning the lottery are small; and even at $100/hour, working harder has its physical limitations. While there's certainly some truth that you must work hard if you desire to earn money, it is also true that money is available and accessible without necessarily *working harder*.

The fact is, **there's not a direct correlation between how hard you work and how much money you make.**

This is especially true if you work for a salary. No matter how hard you work, your earnings will be limited to the amount of your salary (granted, the existence of high-income earners).

There is, however, a direct correlation between your money mindset and how much money you make. That is why some people can do a fraction of the amount of "work" that hard workers do, but make considerably more money.

The way you think about money and what you believe have a real influence on how much income you can generate, as well as how you behave financially.

Your money mindset can do 1 of 2 things:

- Catapult you to wealth
- Keep you in poverty

That's how powerful mindset and beliefs are.

The absence of an effective money mindset equals the inability to reach the level of success you want, which means falling short of maximizing your financial capabilities.

Being trapped in a negative mindset and not knowing how to change is extremely detrimental. Many parents pass down thoughts and beliefs mainly because things have always been done a certain way. So, in effect, children take on the same ways of thinking and are subject to the limitations of said ways.

As examples, I saw my grandfather, my father, my godfather, uncles, and neighbors work as career men. It was the way I saw things done. Without a doubt, I carried (still carry) the utmost respect for those men. They were the fathers of my cousins and friends, and they all contributed to the stability and happiness that I was blessed to enjoy as a child.

After being dealt the hand of tragedy (losing my dad), I felt to some degree, that I was in their shoes. Looking back on those new responsibilities, I can better understand why so many of us live with a strain on our relationship with money:

- **We want more of it,** but can't ever seem to get enough. "…too much month left at the end of the money."

- **We know that money can achieve good things**, but we're tight with spending because it's hard to get. As my dad used to say, **"Money don't grow on trees…"**.

- **We're grateful when we have the money to purchase the things we want**; but other teachings related to values, morals, and religion can make us feel guilty about not giving it away instead. Don't get me wrong. I believe in the importance of having empathy for others and showing compassion. But I'd have to admit that I have felt in times past, that I should be content with settling for less because it was the spiritual thing to do.

How Beliefs Create and Limit Your Financial Reality

Your beliefs are the seeds that create your reality. Your beliefs affect your thoughts, which affect your actions, which ultimately create your life circumstances. *Changing your beliefs can be the most powerful way to alter your life.* Altering your beliefs changes the entire cycle.

There are several ways that beliefs ultimately alter your financial behavior:

1. **Beliefs influence your self-confidence.** The set of beliefs you have about YOU and your capabilities determines your level of self-confidence. In turn, your confidence affects your ability to learn and apply new financial habits.

    - Confidence also impacts your ability to pursue financial goals. If you're not confident in your ability to get results, you won't persevere.

2. **Beliefs alter how you process information.** Scientists have found that people use new information to support beliefs they already possess, rather than to form new beliefs. If you believe that you can't save money, you'll look for evidence to support that belief.

    - Information that is contrary to your beliefs is quickly discarded and ignored. This makes change especially difficult because beliefs have you stuck in your ways.

3. **Beliefs create limits.** It's almost impossible to rise above your beliefs. If you believe that you'll never be wealthy, you're right. If you believe you can't stick to a budget, you're right again. This is why it's so important to change your beliefs to

viewpoints that support, rather than limit, you.

4. **Beliefs affect results.** If you don't think you can have a pleasant retirement, you're unlikely to save or learn about the various types of retirement accounts.

    - If you believe that money changes people for the worse, you won't take the steps to accumulate a significant amount.

Beliefs are the core of financial challenges. *Enhanced beliefs lead to enhanced thoughts, actions, and results.* Attacking your negative *behaviors* is a less effective route to success. Instead, focus on your beliefs and you're more likely to enjoy positive benefits from your efforts.

Negative Money Beliefs

Examples of beliefs that keep you poor:

1. **Rich people are greedy.** Some rich people are indeed greedy. But some poor people are greedy, too. Many rich people became rich through kindness and helping others. *Whether or not you're greedy is up to you.*

2. **I don't deserve to be wealthy.** Everyone that creates value deserves to be wealthy. If you're content with a minimum wage job or spend the day sitting on the couch, you can change your financial circumstances by creating value and charging the world for it.

3. **I'll have to do a lot of things I don't like to become wealthy.** While doing things that others don't like to do can be a faster way to wealth, there are numerous ways to accumulate

wealth. At least one of them would be enjoyable for you.

4. **My friends won't like me if I'm rich.** It's common to find new friends as your life situation evolves. Some of your friends might not like the fact that you're rich. But your true friends will be happy for you. Every change in life has the potential to influence everything else.

    - Many CEOs and other wealthy folks still have the same friends from elementary school. You can choose to do the same.

5. **Money is the root of all evil.** The actual quote is "The love of money is the root of all evil." Money doesn't create negative situations. Money is just a piece of paper or a number attached to a bank account. Money is neutral, not evil.

    - *Money provides opportunity.* It's your choice whether the actions you take are positive or negative.

6. **I can't be spiritual and have a lot of money.** Many religions espouse the belief that being poor is somehow looked upon more kindly by the great powers that be. As I mentioned about myself, I felt that being content with less than I could potentially attain was an expression of spiritual gratefulness.

    - Having money gives you more opportunities to be good to yourself and others. It can also free up your time to engage in more spiritual activities.

7. **I'm disrespecting my parents if I make more money than they do.** Most parents would be proud to see their children do well...even if it's better than they did.

8. **It's hard to make a lot of money.**

    - *With the appropriate habits in place, it's not too difficult to enhance your career, save more, spend less, and invest more wisely.*

    - **Getting rich is hard.** Guess what? ***Being broke is hard too!*** Which hard will win in your life?

9. **If I had a lot of money, I'd probably just lose it anyway.** Keeping money is as much of a skill as earning and saving it. There are plenty of resources that can help you learn how to handle money wisely.

    - The belief that you'll end up where you started will prevent you from taking any meaningful action.

10. **I shouldn't have more money than I need.** Everything in life is easier with a buffer. Imagine having more time and love than you need. Having more money than you "need" is comforting and opens up many possibilities that simply don't exist without a surplus of funds.

    - It's much easier to make a career change or go back to school.
    - You can afford to send your child to Princeton instead of the local community college. (This is only about what you may be able to afford. Attending local community college can be part of a financial strategy).
    - You're better prepared for any financial catastrophe.
    - The belief that you shouldn't have more money than you need to survive will lead to surviving instead of thriving.

Do you have any of these common beliefs about money or yourself? *If you hold beliefs that block your ability to address having a healthy financial situation, you will always go against the grain.* You'll hold yourself back by neglecting the habits necessary to achieve financial happiness.

Is any of this holding you back?
- I'll have plenty of time later.
- I'm too young to worry about it.
- I have to buy a house first.
- I won't live long enough to enjoy it.
- I can't afford to save money now for something I won't need for 40 years.
- It's too complicated for me.
- The amount I'm able to save won't make a difference.

If you want to enhance your finances, eliminating negative beliefs and replacing them with positive beliefs will have to happen within you. To be less technical about it, "Stop blocking your blessings by letting the devil in!" is what my mom would say.

Don't be content with scarcity or lack. Think about all the abundance in the world. Don't let your mind keep you in neutral. Put yourself in drive and go get it! "You can't have faith and be worried about it and doubting at the same time." (mom again).

Whether you believe in God or universal intelligence or the energy behind all things, you must believe that it wants you to prosper. You must not live with a scarcity mindset. And my pet peeve is that you **DON'T WANT THAT MINDSET FOR YOUR CHILDREN (or nieces/nephews)!**

The world is full of abundance, and if you're living in scarcity, then it's time to change your mind about money. To believe that there's enough, that *you* deserve to have money, and that the universe wants you to experience abundance.

Positive Money Beliefs

Some beliefs will speed you along the path to financial independence. These positive habits make it easier to have a positive financial future.

Get in gear with these beliefs:

1. **Money results from providing value to the world.** It doesn't matter how smart or educated you are. It doesn't matter what you look like. If you provide value and charge people for it, you will receive a corresponding level of money. **Do NOT be afraid to profit from solving problems.**

    - Brain surgeons make more money than your average store clerk because the surgeon is providing more value. A CEO of a large corporation earns more than a brain surgeon for the same reason.

2. **Money provides freedom and choice.** Money is great for solving problems and providing YOU with **_options_**. Maybe money can't buy you love, but enough of it can fix a bad transmission, buy a ticket to Dubai, or allow you to play golf while your employees work. It's called buying your time back.

3. **I can help others with my money.** After meeting your needs, how many times have you declared what you would do for your loved ones or friends *IF YOU HAD THE MONEY?*

4. **My financial freedom will happen when I have effective beliefs, thoughts, and habits.** It's not necessary to do anything spectacular. *Simple actions, taken regularly, will result in the accumulation of money. But it all starts with your beliefs.*

5. **Saving money is easy and enjoyable.** How would your savings activities change if you believed this?

6. **A budget is easy to create and follow.** If you can't seem to create or stick with a budget, this belief will help.

7. **I only buy things I need.** How would your bank account look if you lived like this? How would it feel to stop giving your money away to big businesses?

There are numerous others, but you get the idea. ***Do you have more positive or negative beliefs about money?*** Can you see how your beliefs about money are affecting your financial situation?

Your beliefs and focus will determine what you attract.

- Focus on positive things and you'll attract positive things.
- Focus on negative things and you'll attract the negative.

Or as T. Harv Ecker puts it:
> *"Whatever results you're getting, be they rich or poor, good or bad, positive or negative, always remember that your outer world is simply a reflection of your inner world. If things aren't going well in your outer life, it's because things aren't going well in your inner life. It's that simple."*

If you're not experiencing what you want in your life, it's primarily due to what's happening in your inner world.

- Not attracting the wealth you want? Inner world.
- Not able to get your head above water financially? Inner world.
- Not able to move forward in your job the way you should? Inner world.

Thankfully, whether you know it or not, you're the one in control of your inner world.

You determine what you think about and focus on. The more you control and shape your inner world, the more you will control and shape your actual reality. It doesn't have to be amazing, only real to you, and/or a realness that you want your children to experience.

The massive implication is that if you want to change your life and attract more wealth, you absolutely must master the way you think.

Financial Therapy: Gratitude

One of the best ways to choose abundance is through the practice of gratitude. Declare daily what you are thankful for. This will help shape your mood and attitude.

Start practicing gratitude for all the ways that the heavenly father has shown Himself mighty in your life. When you receive something good and positive, say a simple, "Thank you." This practice will start to transform the way you live.

Look at the cycle of gratitude this way. When you're grateful for even the smallest things, positive energy goes forth from you, then attracts more positive things into your life for you to be grateful for. *"What goes around comes around"* is how it was taught to us.

This practice is how I have personally come to control my own morale in life. I don't leave my morale up to anyone but me! And your morale should be controlled by **YOU!**

Positive Money Beliefs in Action

Positive money beliefs are a necessary component of financial therapy. But the beliefs don't work alone. Action **MUST** be taken!

Formula: **Positive Beliefs + Action = Desires Become Reality**

T. Harv Ecker calls this the wealth principle:

Thoughts lead to feelings. Feelings lead to actions. Actions lead to results.

Step 1 of "How to Fix Broke": Get your mind right!

Step 1: Action Exercise #1 Goal Setting

In the context of financial therapy and managing personal finance, your baseline about money will be centered around earning, spending, saving, investing, and protection.

The first step is to write down your desires and goals. Be as specific as possible when writing them down. You want to be so specific that you can see them in your mind's eye.

Ask yourself questions like:

1. What do I want to get out of life?
2. What are my biggest dreams?
3. What do I want to accomplish?
4. How much money do I want to make?
5. When do I want to make it by?
6. What example do I want to set for my children?
7. What do I need to learn so I can teach them?

The more concrete you can be when writing down your desires and goals, the more you'll be able to visualize them coming true.

The more you can visualize them, the more positive emotion you'll feel around them and the more focused you'll be on them.

And the more focused you are on your desires, the more you'll attract them into your life.

Say things like:

- "I affirm (believe) that I am going to increase my income by XX date."
- "I affirm (declare) that I am a financial success in all areas of my life."
- "I affirm (speak into existence) that this is my best year ever financially."

Even if you don't know how these things are going to happen, affirm that they will. Affirmations create positive energy around you that will keep you motivated and on track.

You will find out that it works only after you've tried it.

Step 1: Action Exercise #2 Goal Setting Actions

Once you've written down your desires and goals, it's crucial to start taking action on them every day.

What do you need to do in order to make your dreams a reality? Don't worry if you don't have this all figured out. Just begin taking action on whatever is in your heart and on your mind.

- Do you need to call someone?
- Hire a mentor?
- Start building another business on the side?
- Send an email to an important contact?
- Call a friend you haven't spoken to in a while?

If you have an abundance mindset and are open to the possibilities of the universe, actions will begin to pop into your mind. You'll start to have ideas that you didn't have before. Creativity from the inner you will become opportunities for the outer you.

When ideas are impressed upon you, take action!

The more you take action, the more impressive the results you'll see. You'll genuinely realize that you have true potential. You'll achieve things you never believed were possible.

It's Your Future

And now for the million-dollar question: **what are you going to do with your life?**

You now know that:

- You truly have potential.
- Most of the myths you've believed about money are false.
- Your inner thoughts control your outer reality.
- You have the power to shape your reality.
- You can attract and manifest the wealth and dreams that you desire.
- The universe has your back and is supporting your dreams.

Are you going to start taking action to achieve your goals? Or are you going to continue living asleep at the wheel, walking through life mostly unconscious of what you can achieve?

Are you going to take control of your destiny, master your money mindset, and achieve your dreams, or are you going to continue struggling?

The future can be amazing for you if you choose to seize it.
Don't let that future pass you by. Don't arrive 30 years from now and regret the actions that you didn't take.

STEP 2: MAKE MONEY

As time passed, opportunities presented themselves; and I decided to move on from the loading dock. I'll share later how I kept my head up and played my (Spades) hand.

The men that I looked up to were working men. They were not slothful. They were stand-up men who took care of business. So, I understood that getting money meant that I had to work for it.

At 10 and 11 years old, cutting grass or washing cars in the neighborhood were ways to make money; but my neighbors and I were a close group of friends growing up. We would wash cars and cut grass together for no pay at all most of the time. None of us were concerned about not eating.

We were all tasked with keeping our yards presentable. The big jobs we would help each other do. But the idea of us forming a lawn care service or carwash never came up.

Once I was old enough to work a job, that's what I did to make money. After marriage and the births of two children, more money meant getting another job. Again, it's what I knew to do. At one point, my job made way for me to work regular overtime, which was essentially a second job with much better pay. Time and a half was a pretty good rate!

As my children (now young adults) were growing, I started teaching them that having a job and making money are two different things. "You're too young to get jobs; but not too young to make money", is what I would say. By middle and high school, they were taking advantage of being able to earn not paychecks, but profits!

Types of Income:

There are 3 types of income to earn in the United States. Capitalism, our economic system, makes this possible.

1. *Earned*: the exchange of your time for money; earned income that requires you to be present to get paid

2. *Portfolio:* capital gains from stocks, bonds, and market investments

3. *Passive:* income that you don't work for; your money works for you; earn money while you sleep

To put the 3 income types in context, consider this:

1. *Earned:* an employee at McDonald's earns a wage/salary

2. *Portfolio:* an owner of McDonald's stocks earns income from the payout of dividends

3. *Passive:* an owner of a McDonald's franchise earns money without working there

The beautiful part about capitalism is that we can earn money in all three ways simultaneously. You can work, own stocks, and own a business at the same time. It doesn't have to be done that way, but it is possible.

Additionally, there are four methods of earning income.

4 Methods of Earning Income:

1. **Employee or W-2:** job earning a wage or salary (cashier, nurse, engineer, city worker)
2. **Self-employment:** own your job (truck owner operator, lawyer, contractor, dentist)
3. **Business owner:** (big) business that sells products and services (500+ employees) or small business.
4. **Investor:** payouts from real estate, stocks, businesses you started or purchased

The methods of earning income were made popular by Robert Kiyosaki's teaching of the Cash Flow Quadrant. As it relates to personal finance, the take-away is to know that the method by which you earn determines the method by which you are taxed. Active income earned as a wage/salary or W-2 status is the most heavily taxed, which can make taxes a working person's biggest expense.

Since the other earning methods are not taxed as aggressively, it is wise to explore means of earning additional income via a business as opposed to working a second job. This is not to say that working a 2nd job is ineffective when it comes to fulfilling financial obligations or meeting goals. I have personally gone to the extent of working 2 full-time jobs in the past. However, the tax obligation from income earned through self-employment or from being an investor or business owner is much lighter on the bank account than being a W-2.

Think of all the ways that you can earn money. Revisit the four methods of earning money, which are legal, moral, and ethical; and take action that will help you earn most effectively.

In addition, if you have children who are not old enough to get a job, teach them that they can create and act on money-making ideas from their bedrooms or the kitchen table at home.

The idea is to educate and empower children early in life to make business decisions, using real currency. I've had one main point to get across to my children: **Profits are better than wages.**

Step 2 Exercise: Personal Earning Exploration

Are you passionate about your work? **It can be much easier to be successful financially and professionally if you can combine your passions and your work.**

Most of us play it safe and choose a career or create a business based largely on practicality. After all, it's easier to find work as an accountant than as an artist. Technology was the field that I chose in order to get back indoors!

But it's possible to have both.

Your answers to these questions will help you discover your passions:

- What do I like to do in my free time?

- What part of my current job would I be willing to do for free?

- When did I last have a hard time sleeping because I was so excited?

- What would I do if I had unlimited time and resources?

- As a child, what did I want to be when I grew up?

- What issues in the world are most important to me?

- What is my greatest talent?

- What would I be if I could be anything?

- What is exciting to me?

- What do people thank me for?

- What are my 3 most important core values?

- Who do I look up to?

- When do I consistently over-deliver?

- On which topics am I willing to debate and argue?

- What makes me come alive?

- When I go to the bookstore, where do I spend most of my time?

- What do I want to be remembered for?

- Which worldwide challenge would I solve if I could?

- What do my friends think would be the perfect job for me?

As you answer all these questions, you'll likely recognize a recurring theme that points to your passion.

Applying yourself in an area you're passionate about will do wonders for your business, career, and finances.

Be assured too, that passion points are also pain points. So not doing what you passionately want to do can deeply harm you.

STEP 3: PAY YOURSELF FIRST

Referred to by some as the *"golden rule of personal finance"*, this concept can be the difference-maker regarding your working life and retirement. Or it can determine your earning status: ie: employee, business owner, or investor

A simple breakdown:
- *Personal = My*
- *Finance = Money*

Personal Finance = My Money

My money is valuable to me!
My time is valuable to me!
My efforts are valuable to me!
It is with this thought process that I easily pay myself first. When I think of how early in the mornings I've gotten up for work, how long I've sat in traffic, or how many times I've missed events because I've had to work, I most definitely pay myself first. It is a definite money belief that I have put into action.

The habit of paying myself first while working on the loading dock paid off. I set a goal to save $10K. Although I didn't reach that goal before moving on to another job, the habit of saving that way helped fund the down payment on my first home at 23 years old. I found a way to make the Queen of Clubs bring me a book!

I state for the sake of clarity, that I am addressing this concept in the context of net (or bring home) pay! Yes, there is a place for 401K, IRA, and other retirement savings. But those are generally not funded with "bring home" funds.
(Note: ROTH IRAs and Annuities are funded with bring-home funds.)

The tip refers to the practice of saving some of your money before you pay any of your bills.

Ideally, the money is taken out of your paycheck before you ever see it and is deposited into some sort of investment or savings account. A high yield account is ideal, but no longer traditional.

It might seem that you could just as easily pay your bills and then save the leftover money, but that rarely works. What commonly happens is your lifestyle expands to the amount in your bank account. You'll pay your bills and there will be nothing left. So, think of it this way, a portion of all the money you make should be yours to keep. Get that portion before anyone else does.

By paying yourself first, you'll find that you adjust your lifestyle accordingly and save money a little more easily. The practice should be to live off less than what you take home.

Pay Yourself First: How to Do It and Why

1. **Set up your automatic savings.** You have two options available to you: either have the money taken out of your paycheck or have your checking account set up for automatic payment.

   - Larger employers will allow you to have a part of your paycheck deposited directly into a separate account. This should be an investment account of some sort. Having a 401K is most commonly how this is done. This is a good thing because you're paying your future, older self.

But what about saving for other purposes like buying a home, starting a business, or taking advantage of an investment opportunity?

- You can also set up your checking account to auto-pay a set amount on a specific date every month. Similarly, you could have your savings account auto-debit the amount each month. *Just be sure not to spend the money before your savings 'bill' gets paid. Your savings 'bill' is a payment to YOU!*

Keep in mind that you can do this with multiple accounts. If your employer can divert part of your paycheck to another account, they can break it up further and send part of your money to your checking account, part to your investment account, and another part to a third account. Not to mention what you can set up on your own, aside from doing it through your employer.

- If you're self-employed, then the method of auto-debiting your checking account is the way to go.

2. **How much should I pay myself? How much should I save?** These questions present psychological challenges for some because they feel like they don't earn enough to save anything. **This is rarely true.** In workshops and personal coaching sessions I've facilitated, I've found that people have expenses that they are simply not willing to do without. Remember from the financial therapy chapter that actions follow mindset. Are you of the mindset that Hulu, Netflix, and the cable company are all more deserving of your money than you? Do you value the products of restaurants and burger joints more than you value your money on every payday? The unwillingness to make those changes, even for as little as 90 days is what holds a lot of people back.
Examine your spending and see if you can free up some funds. We'll discuss this more in the next step.

Pay yourself first funds can be as much as 40% of bring home pay. But there is no rule. Simply commit to an amount that you can save consistently. Some couples save the entire income of one person and live off the income of the other person. If you are doubtful, start saving 1%. You won't feel the pain of saving 1% of your paycheck, especially if your value system is in check. The next month save 2%. Keep increasing the amount for as long as you can. You're doing well if you can get up to 10%. You're doing great if you can get up to 20% or more! Most importantly, develop the habit.

- Whenever you pay off a debt, consider adding that money to your savings. Simply keep making the payments, only now you can make them to yourself.

It is important to emphasize that "pay yourself first" funds are for affording yourself the option to invest should opportunities arise. Also, emergency funds can be started via "pay yourself first".

Pay yourself first contributions are not for the following examples:

- holiday shopping
- vacation spending
- big-screen TVs
- wardrobes

Such items are addressed in the next step.

The key is to get the money out of your hands as quickly as possible. Ideally, you'd never have possession of the money in your checking account. Save automatically and you will create options for yourself in the future.

"Save a part of your income and begin now, for the man with a surplus controls circumstances, and the man without a surplus is controlled by circumstances."
- Henry Buckley

STEP 4: TAKE CONTROL OF YOUR FINANCES

Regardless of your income, you can gain control of your financial life and look forward to a secure future. All you need is a clear plan – based on your own circumstances – to guide you to financial stability.

In the introduction, it was mentioned that you will move into the Action Stage of Behavior Change while going through this book. This chapter is a guide that will immediately start turning your positive money beliefs into action. Over the next four weeks (or faster if you'd like), you will outline a plan to take control of your finances, which will put you on a path towards monetary success.

Week 1: Create a Budget

Creating a realistic, workable budget that you can commit to is the cornerstone of any plan to gain control of your finances. A good budget helps you to accomplish many objectives:

- Record and track expenses and income
- Plan for unexpected events
- Identify areas that challenge you to keep spending on track
- Set and achieve financial goals

A budget is a TOOL. It is best used to track where your money goes and to find opportunities to put money back on the table. Follow these easy steps to create your own budget and begin the process of gaining greater control over your money:

1. **Identify and list all sources of income.** The first step in deciding how to spend or save your money is to determine how much income you have coming in.

    - Begin by listing all of your sources of income, including the amount and frequency that you receive your payments.

    - Income includes any money that you receive in the form of wages or payment for work, as well as money from irregular sources such as windfalls, inheritances, yard sales, rebates, or even refunds.

2. **Identify and list all of your expenses.** Determine your expenses, their type, and their frequency. *It's impossible to control your expenses without first identifying them.*

The two most common categories of expenses are fixed and variable:

- **Fixed expenses.** Fixed expenses reoccur on a frequent, regular basis. Your mortgage or rent payments, life, auto, or health insurance premiums, and vehicle payments are common fixed expenses. Also, remember any other installment loans

- **Variable expenses.** Variable expenses can occur infrequently or regularly, but the amount is typically sporadic or varies. Examples of variable expenses include your monthly utilities, grocery bills, gifts, overdraft charges, and children's school activities. *These expenses are harder to estimate, but they're an important part of a workable budget.*

3. **Plan your budget.** Once you've identified your income and expenses, you can begin to plan how to you'll spend your money and meet your financial goals. Just as each person is a unique individual with talents of their own, abilities, and preferences, *each person's budget and financial goals are unique.* Despite this, there are some general rules and practices that everyone can use to increase their financial stability.

    - In general, you'll want to save a portion of your income and use it to meet any number of common financial goals.

    - Common financial goals that will increase your financial security and peace of mind include: building a savings fund for emergencies, paying off debt, saving for short and long-term needs, retirement planning, investments, and so forth.

- ***It's important to leave room in your budget for fun or unplanned expenses.*** Just like a diet to lose weight, if your plan is too strict, you are likely to cheat and not stick to it in the long term.

- When planning how much of your income to spend, save, and invest, take the time to ***identify any areas that challenge you.*** For instance, if you find that you frequently go over your budget for groceries, develop a plan to rein in costs at the grocery store.

- Identify areas of your spending that you can cut back on to fund your savings and investment plans. Also, ***look for ways you can boost your income to add to your savings.***

4. **Automate common budgeting tasks to help eliminate boredom.** You are unlikely to stick to your budget if the process consumes too much of your time.

    - There are numerous free and low-cost budgeting software programs available online. ***Take advantage of these tools to make budgeting and controlling your finances easier and more enjoyable.***

5. **Keep your budget updated with frequent reviews.** By keeping your budget relevant to your current situation, you can ensure that you aren't caught unawares of changes in your income or expenses.

You will not nail a budget on the first take. Try different approaches based on your pay cycle and bill due dates. Consider reverse budgeting to meet savings goals. If you want to save $5000 in six months, divide 5000 by 6 and get the monthly bill you should pay to your account. Take this thought into next week.

"A good financial plan is a road map that shows us exactly how the choices we make today will affect our future."
- Alexa Von Tobel

Week 2: Establish a Savings Plan

We discussed in a previous chapter, the concept of "pay yourself first". Therefore, your very first payment should be made out to the bill of **YOU**. This practice has several advantages and serves multiple constructive purposes. Additional savings, however, can be strategically worked into your budget.

Consider the benefits of building your savings:

- Savings free you from various sources of stress, such as the worry that comes from living paycheck to paycheck and wondering if you have enough saved for retirement.

- Stressing out over your lack of savings takes a toll on your physical and emotional well-being, and can lead to arguments and strife with loved ones. Saving helps you feel more secure, less stressed and can strengthen your relationships with family members. Think of the people you could mentor mainly because you have savings protocol in place.

- Savings can give you the freedom to get more enjoyment out of life. Saving money makes it easier to take vacations or have funds available to pursue your hobbies and educational goals.

Do not panic if you haven't started saving to reach your financial goals. It is not uncommon. According to the Financial Security

Index Chart created by Bankrate: 75% of Americans don't have enough savings to cover at least 6 months of their expenses, and 27% have $0 in emergency savings. Be assured though, that all is not lost. It's never too late to start building your savings!

During the week after you've gotten an initial budget in place, use these strategies to increase your savings and begin to reap the benefits:

1. **Identify your savings goals.** Savings goals can be grouped into three categories: short, medium, and long-term goals.

   - **Common short-term savings goals can normally be achieved in less than 12 months.** Examples include establishing a $500 emergency fund to cover unexpected repairs or costs, saving for a vacation, or saving for a down payment on a new car.

   - **Medium-term savings goals normally take at least one or more years to accomplish.** Examples include saving at least 6 months of your living expenses to protect you should you lose your job, saving the money for a down payment on a home, or saving a sum to pay down debt.

   - **Long-range savings goals take many years to fully fund.** Examples include saving for your retirement or the future college tuition of your children or grandchildren.

2. **Plan to meet your goals.** As you create each savings goal, *design a workable plan that will enable you to begin making it a reality.*

- Ideally, you will create separate accounts for each savings goal. Savings for short-term goals should be kept in funds that are easy to get to, such as a standard savings account at a bank.

- Medium and long-term savings goals can be invested in ways that will help the balance to grow over a longer period of time, such as CDs, mutual funds, annuities, stocks, and bonds.

- Increasing your savings, especially in the long term, sometimes means exposing the initial investment to some risk. As you near the time frame for completion of your goal, you'll want to reduce your risk and also make it easier to access those funds.

3. **Increasing your savings means changing your spending patterns and behavior.** Most of the time, you can find the necessary funds to increase your savings by exercising greater control over your spending. *Reducing your spending on variable expenses is a great place to start!*

    - Look for ways to reduce wasteful and unnecessary spending. Eliminate subscriptions to newspapers and magazines that you infrequently read and **cut back on services** for your cable TV and home telephone. Contact your carriers and seek discounts for bundled services.

    - Contact your insurance and banking companies and see if you are eligible for discounts based on your customer status and your club or group affiliations.

    - Contact your electric company and ask for a free energy audit of your home to identify areas where you can reduce your consumption and lower your electric bill. ***Follow their advice and save money by plugging leaks and installing energy-efficient appliances.***

- Reduce your food bill by eating at restaurants less often and eliminating fast food meals. Coffee, beverages, and most meals are nearly always less expensive when they are prepared from whole foods at home.

- You can further reduce your food bill by searching for grocery store coupons online and combining them with loss leaders and daily specials. For the greatest savings, plan your meals around foods that are on sale.

- ***Once you begin to critically examine how you are spending your income, you will surprise yourself at all of the ingenious ways you discover to save money!***

4. **Boost your savings by increasing your income.** Reducing your expenses is only half of the equation. It may also be necessary to increase your income in order to meet your savings goals. More details about increasing your income follow later in this guide.

5. **Start saving early.** While it's certainly true that it's never too late to start saving, the sooner you start, the longer period of time you'll have to allow the power of compound interest to effortlessly grow your savings.

By spending the second week of your 4-week plan on discovering ways to build your savings, you're well on your way to escaping financial duress.

Week 3: Plan to Eliminate Debt

First and foremost, debt is the #1 killer of wealth. Just figure earning $1.00 then spending $1.25 due to interest and fees. Throughout human history, uncontrolled, unsustainable levels of debt have led to the destruction of both individual households and entire countries. The most recent recession in the United States began in 2008, and the cause can be partly attributed to too much debt.

One of the biggest drawbacks to acquiring debt is the interest that makes it difficult to pay off. Most forms of debt involve interest, so the balance is constantly growing. Making debt payments also takes away from the money you might otherwise get to spend on things such as home repairs, clothing, or increasing your savings.

Reducing the amount of your debt increases your financial security. When you pay off your debt, you have more money to put towards savings or pay your other expenses more easily should you experience an unexpected drop in your income.

Use these debt-reducing strategies during the third week of your plan to achieve greater financial security:

1. **List your debts.** Make a list of all of your debts and include the interest rates and the amount and frequency of payments for each one.

    - Ensure that you've budgeted enough funds to cover your minimum payments so you avoid late fees, additional charges, and damage to your credit rating.

- Late payments can damage your credit score and make it more difficult to obtain future credit as well as increase the interest rate that you must pay.

2. **Decide on a debt repayment strategy that you can stick to.** There are a few well-known strategies for paying off debt, but only you can decide which one will work best for your personal situation.

    - A common debt repayment strategy is to focus your efforts on paying down the credit card or account with the highest balance and interest rate first. Once this account is paid off, you then take the amount you were paying on this account and add it to the minimum payment of your next debt account. This is called the avalanche method.

    - If you have several smaller debts, it may make more sense to focus your efforts on paying off one or two of these smaller amounts very quickly and then adding the payments from these accounts to those with a larger balance. The is debt the snowball method. This was my method of choice during my financial recovery. I am also an alum of Dave Ramsey's Financial Coach Master Training program. The debt snowball is effective.

    - *Regardless of the amount that you owe, most financial experts advise against taking funds from your retirement or other long-term savings accounts to fund debt repayment.*

- If you can't find money in your current budget to use to pay off your debt, look for ways to increase your income rather than raiding your retirement accounts. Do NOT liquidate retirement funds to pay off debt.

- Continue to save towards your other financial goals while you work on paying off your debt. In this way, your savings have a longer span of time to take advantage of compound interest and long-term trends in the bond and stock markets.

3. **Once you are out of debt, plan to use that money to help you achieve your financial goals.** Rather than splurging on unnecessary expenses, or going back into debt, take the money that you no longer need to spend on debt repayment and use it to increase your savings or purchase long-term assets that increase your wealth.

- *Learning to plan for repairs and common expenses, and creating a savings plan for these items, can help you to stay out of debt.*

Uncontrolled debt is dangerous to your wealth and financial security. Whenever part of your income is tied up with the servicing of your debt, you're more susceptible to the negative effects of income reductions and price increases for products and services that you need. Inflation and debt are a bad combination when it comes to your money. Everything is going up in price; so, driving down debt is the offensive plan for freeing up money.

The tables below are excerpts from a budgeting case study.

Casual Monthly Expenses	
Cable / Satellite	$375
Gym Membership	$35
Weekend Cocktails	$140
Monthly Get-Away	$360
Club Dues	$150
Subscriptions	$120
Total	**$1,180**

Monthly Debt Payments / Balances		
Item	Amount	Balance
Credit Card #1	$20	$1,150
Credit Card #2	$30	$2,700
Credit Card #3	$55	$4,600
IRS Payment Plan	$100	$4,000
Auto Loan #1	$350	$11,450
Auto Loan #2	$455	$15,500
Total	**$1,010**	**$39,400**

Notice the itemized designations for their income. We consider these to be examples of *giving away* their hard-earned money to big businesses. Lifestyle changes from the first table can be used to eliminate debt in the second illustration.

While it is not the intent of EFI to impose our will on anyone's choices, it is important to point out that where your money goes is indicative of where your values lie.

If you are not sure of how to start budgeting for life's necessities, savings, and debt, see the **income allocation strategies** below:

A: 80|20 80% Expenses 20% Savings / Debt	**B: 50|30|20** 50% Expenses 30% Wants 20% Savings / Debt
C: 70|10|10|10 70% Expenses 10% Savings 10% Invest 10% Charitable Giving	**D: 75|15|10** 75% Expenses 15% Invest 10% Savings

The percentages in the chart are not rules. They are suggestions to help with managing your income to address your needs, goals, and desires.

If circumstances change while you address debt balances, and you find yourself under a financial strain, do not fret over who to pay or what to sacrifice. Always prioritize the:
Four Walls of Survival:
- Housing (including utilities)
- Food
- Transportation (including insurance)
- Clothing

I know that making a financial recovery is not done in 30 days. Be reminded that this is 4 weeks of initial planning and the start of developing habits that will help you reach your goals. The length of time will vary from person to person.

> *"Debt can turn a free, happy person into a bitter human being."*
> *- Michael Mihalik*

Week 4: Increase Income

For most of us, the final step to achieving our financial goals lies in finding ways to increase our income. This is because we've addressed behavioral habits and tendencies in the previous steps.

When you increase your income, it logically follows that as long as you keep your expenses the same, or reduce them, you'll have more money to achieve most financial goals, including:
- increasing your savings
- paying down your debt
- increasing your investments
- saving for retirement
- acquiring debt-free assets
- creating additional revenue streams

Increasing income, however, is often easier said than done. After the financial shocks of the last several years, many employers are reluctant to increase the salaries of their workers. For most, less overtime and fewer bonuses are available, so it's difficult to increase your income if you rely solely on your paycheck.

During the fourth week of your 4-week plan, consider these ways to boost your income:

1. **Sell items you don't need or use infrequently.** Examples include selling a second car that you rarely use or having a

yard sale for items you no longer want, like gently used children's clothing, electronics, and common household items and gadgets.

- *For best results, be certain to save, rather than spend, the proceeds from your sales.*

2. **Consider taking on a part-time job, even if it's just on a temporary or seasonal basis.** By increasing your income with a second job, you can obtain the funds necessary to achieve your financial goals.

3. **Look for ways to turn your hobbies into a secondary source of income.** Do you have a hidden talent, such as woodworking, singing, or drawing? Look for ways to use these skills to sell products or services related to your hobby.

   - *You could also teach or demonstrate your skills to pick up some extra dollars.*

4. **Create multiple lines of passive income streams.** Use some of your savings to buy investments that produce a passive income stream, such as buying a property that will produce rental income.

   - *If you are great at selling, market the products of others for a share of the sales.* Green products and cleaning supplies, clothing, jewelry, and decor are just some examples of products where you can earn a commission when you sell their products.

10 Ideas for Boosting Your Income

There are plenty of opportunities to boost your income if you're willing to hustle. *A few hours each week can add significantly to your discretionary income.* You'll find a few ideas listed below, but come up with a list of your own ideas. With enough creativity, you might discover an untapped source of secondary income.

Boost your income starting tomorrow:

1. **Be a part-time personal assistant.** You can make phone calls, run errands, mow the grass, have the car washed, or pick up the kids. Think of all the things you wish you had help with. You can provide that to someone else. *While there aren't too many people that can use an assistant full-time, there are many people that could use an hour or two of help.*

2. **Rent your car.** How much time do you actually spend driving it? The rest of the time it's just sitting in the driveway dripping oil and serving as a target for birds. Some apps will allow you to list and rent your car. Parking spotter and Relay rides are two examples.

3. **Knock on doors.** A variety of organizations are looking for people to canvas neighborhoods and solicit donations or spread information. You can brush up on your social skills, too.

4. **Bartender.** With the right position, you can make a lot of money quickly. Take a class and learn how to mix your favorite drinks.

5. **Clean houses.** Some people actually like to clean. If you're one of them, you're in luck! Some people are too busy to clean and have the financial resources to pay someone else to do it. All you have to do is find each other. A few basic cleaning supplies are enough to get started.

6. **Housesit.** *If you spend your evenings in front of the TV or playing on your computer anyway, do it at someone else's house and get paid for it.* There's not much to do besides getting the mail.

7. **Teach.** Do you know yoga, algebra, or how to play the violin? Share your knowledge for a price. Use online classifieds or hand out a few fliers. Just a couple of students can provide a nice boost to your income.

8. **Get a roommate.** Split the rent and utilities. That can easily be upwards of $1,000 per month. All you have to do is give up some privacy and half the refrigerator. Be sure to take a shower before the hot water is gone.

9. **Pet-sitter or dog walker.** Pet sitters make around $25 per day. If you're lucky enough to get a good dog, it's an easy job. Dog walkers earn around $15 per 30-minute walk. A few clients can add to your income nicely. Look at rover.com.

10. **Buy and sell things on Craigslist.** People have traded their way from a used cell phone to a Porsche without spending a dime. Look for things selling at a low price. Purchase it and resell at a higher, more reasonable price.

    - There are always good deals to be found. You must be knowledgeable of the item, however. Do you know the typical price for a 1988 USA Peavey Predator guitar? Know the market value of what you're buying and look for someone willing to do something silly.

A little extra income never hurt anyone. Think of other ways to boost your income. *If you're willing to work, you can create a second income that makes a big difference in your life.* Find something that interests you and you'll enjoy yourself more. Many of these tips can be put into action immediately.

Use the *Take Control of Your Finances* checklist to help track your progress.

Take Control of Your Finances: Checklist

Week 1: Budgeting

☐ Identify and list all sources of income.

☐ Identify and list all of your expenses.

☐ Plan how you'll spend your money and meet your financial goals.

☐ Automate common budgeting tasks to help eliminate boredom.

☐ Keep your budget updated with frequent reviews.

Week 2: Building Savings

☐ Identify your savings goals: short, medium, and long term goals

☐ Design a workable plan to change your spending patterns to meet your goals.

☐ Boost your savings by increasing your income.

☐ Start saving early.

Week 3: Paying Off Debt

- ☐ List your debts.
- ☐ Decide on a debt repayment strategy that you can stick to.
- ☐ Once you are out of debt, plan to use that money to help you achieve your financial goals.

Week 4: Increasing Income

- ☐ Sell assets you don't need or use infrequently.
- ☐ Consider taking on a part-time job, even if it's just on a temporary or seasonal basis.
- ☐ Look for ways to turn your hobbies into a secondary source of income.
- ☐ Create multiple lines of passive income streams.

Follow Your New Plans and Live the Life You Dream Of

- ☐ Use 2 days to fine-tune your plans.
- ☐ Start taking action to follow your plans.
- ☐ Anticipate challenges and plan appropriate action.
- ☐ Review your plans periodically and adjust as needed to account for revised goals, new circumstances, or just to make them more workable for you.

STEP 5: PUT YOUR MONEY TO WORK

I want you to ask yourself, out loud… *"When was the last time I bought something that MADE ME MONEY?"* Ponder the thought. Congratulations if spending for a return on your money is common practice for you! However, if you cannot recall a time or have seldom spent money for a return, then engage in this chapter.

Answering the opening question exposes the roots of financial success or financial despair across generations, based on what has been taught, along with what has been adopted as a financial belief system. It points out that we are primarily a society of consumers. Always consuming sends money out, never to be seen again, while investing sends your money out to return with more money.

In workshops that I've conducted, answers to the question, "When was the last time you bought something that made you money?" revealed that a lot of spending habits result in buying **liabilities** *(things that take money out of one's pockets).* The opposite action would be to buy **assets** *(things that put money into one's pockets*). Choosing to buy liabilities versus buying assets is a behavior that has been passed down from generation to generation. For example, if a working person or couple qualifies for a $500,000 mortgage loan, then they will probably have a pretty nice home (at least in Atlanta and surrounding areas. Prices are rising at this very moment though). The choice is made to max out the limits of income to acquire that home (instead of a smaller dwelling). A multi-family dwelling can be acquired for the same amount, which potentially turns a mortgage (liability) into rental income (asset).

On a less expensive note, I engaged my children with a discussion about paying to watch cable television. They were 14 and 11 at the time. I shared with them that the cable/internet bill had gotten to be $160/month. The conversation was driven by the following:

- **How much is $160/month annually?** *"$1920.00"*
- **What do we get in return from the cable company?** *"more shows"*
- **Are the shows more valuable to you than $1920?** *" ...guess not " / "no"*
- **Would you rather share $1920 or more shows?** *"$1920"*
- **What can you do with $160 per month to actually receive money in return?**

Their thoughts flowed from T-shirts to cameras for photography and video editing, to jewelry, and a range of other business ideas.

My point was to let them know that **THEY** were more valuable to me than the cable company when it came down to who received $160 every month. It could have been a greater or lesser amount of money, but I chose to fund opportunities for my children over funding profits for the cable company. It was not about what I could afford. It was about stack ranking what I valued most and putting my money where my heart was (is). They, in turn, leveled up their thinking and became more conscientious about spending for returns on their money.

What one CHOOSES to do with income is arguably the number one factor in personal finance that determines growth, stagnation, or loss. *We will ALL have a legacy*. What will yours be?

If we take the position that money is left over after monthly obligations are met, then putting those dollars to work is the next step. Money left over after monthly bills are paid is referred to as **CASH FLOW**. For a long time, I considered money left over after bills were paid to be **"my discretionary funds"**. As I matured, I came to understand that *fixing broke entails using cash flow to purchase assets that will produce more cash flow.* I've learned to call that cycle, **CASH-ASSETS-CASH**.

Why Should I Invest?

Listed below are three reasons why one should invest.

Preserve Buying Power: The state of money declining in value from year to year is called inflation. It means that on one hand, the costs of goods and services are always increasing; and on the other hand, your paycheck is not. It also means that money you have in the bank or under the mattress will be worth less next year than what it's worth today. For example, your $100 shopping budget buys fewer groceries this year than it bought last year. So your dollar buys less because it's not worth as much. To add perspective, the year I graduated from high school, 1992, the cost of a #1 Combo at McDonald's or Burger King was $2.99. The same year, a gallon of gas was $0.89. Today, the same Big Mac or Whopper is considerably smaller, with the combo costing twice as much; and a gallon of Regular Unleaded is $3.29. The rate of inflation is approaching 3% per year. The idea of investing is to get returns on your money that are higher than the rate of inflation. This helps preserve buying power.

Grow Your Money: By investing, you can grow your money with the accumulation of interest that compounds. When earned interest continuously earns interest, your money grows at a much greater rate than inflation. Albert Einstein labeled compound interest as the 8th Wonder of the World.

In January 2016, I opened a CD at my credit union. It was $5000 for 18 months. By January 2017, the amount earned was $20. Through the banking system, my $5000 worked for me at a return of $1.11 per month. That was a poor and disheartening return on $5000. Think of all the things you could do over a year and a half with $5000. It should be very motivating to think that you could earn more than $1.11 per month with that amount. The rate of return did not compete with the rate of inflation. While this is not an example of the best returns, it's a statement to not let your money just sit in a bank account. Savers literally become losers with inflation being around 3%, and bank products only paying .015%. This will not grow your money or your net worth.

Fund Your Future: On average, we have two stages of adult life: Working years and retirement years. There should be a plan during working years to invest and grow money so that you will not have to work as a senior citizen. 401Ks, Annuities, and IRAs are commonly used as vehicles to grow money for retirement. However, investing in businesses is another way to get a return on your money. It doesn't have to be limited to the exchange market.

Am I Ready to Invest?
Use the following criteria to gauge your readiness to invest.

Do I know my goals? What do I want to get out of investing?
- Saving for retirement?
- Looking to purchase a home?
- Saving for children's/grandchildren's college?

Do I have savings? Having savings ensures that you don't have to deplete funds from investment projects to address emergencies. An emergency fund of 3-6 months of expenses plus a cushion of $750 - $1000 is worth considering to have on hand.

Do I have debt? Assess your debt situation. My recommendation is that any debt that carries interest rates over 7 or 8 percent should be addressed before allocating funds for investing. It doesn't add up to earn 7 or 8 percent on your money while spending 15 -25 percent in credit card interest.

How Can I Start Investing?

It's been five years since I committed $5K to a credit union CD for 18 months. It paid a whopping $1.11 per month for a total of about $20. I used that experience to introduce my children to the importance of earning quality returns. In fact, I used only 2% of that CD amount to fund their first business startup. Yes, with $100 I acquired products for their business. To say the returns are exponentially higher would be a sad joke. To make it plain, they make way more than $1.11 per month. Of course, my own business project was funded as well. A business is an investment consideration, be it your own or another's. I say bet on you.

Investing is an extremely broad subject, but the main idea is to get a return. My first investment was in an IT certification, which qualified me for higher earnings on my job. More specifically, I was able to perform job duties that paid higher wages after investing in myself. Always invest in yourself.

Determine if you want to be an **active** or **passive** investor.
A simple example:
If you acquire a car for $5000, then sell that car for $7500, you've earned an **active** return of $2500.

If you entrust $5000 to a third party to acquire a car, then sell that car for $7500, you may perhaps receive a **passive** return of $1500 due to $1000 service charges from the third party:
$7500 - $5000 - $1000 = $1500.

Another example is in real estate. You can be a landlord who actively screens applicants, collects rents, and fields phone calls from tenants. Or you can choose to be passive and hire a management company to perform all the aforementioned tasks.

As an **active** investor, you spend the necessary time and do most of the legwork required for your investment to go live. You then capture all or most of the returns. As a **passive** investor, you spend very little time doing much less work; but you forfeit some of the returns to fees or charges of the person or company you've agreed to transact business with.

Technology has eased the pain of doing transactions in the market. There are multiple platforms with opportunities to ***actively*** or ***passively*** participate in investing.

This is a brief illustration of how I simplified getting started in the stock market. My teenagers were introduced to buying stocks with the following points and questions?

1. Digital Apps make it easier than ever before. You can now buy fractional shares without having to buy a whole stock. (Stash, Robinhood, Cash App, Webull)
2. Consider products or brands that are used in your home.
3. Is the manufacturer of those brands profitable?
4. What industries or companies are involved in the makeup of the products? (Materials; ie: plastic, metal, batteries, silicon, rubber, wires, computer chips) Look up those manufacturers. Their stocks may be worth purchasing.
5. Are dividends paid by the prospective company to shareholders?

These questions are not advice on how to buy stocks. Neither are they intended to advise you on what shares to buy. It's simply a list of considerations given to two teenagers. It comes down to your investing goals and objectives.

My goal is to pay small bills (home security system, internet, cell phones) with dividends or other *non-wage* income.

Scenario:

I wanted to treat myself to a $450 item for my birthday (2020). After an internal battle of going back and forth, I decided against it. I **CHOSE** instead, to invest the $450. I broke down the transaction of what I would purchase from the point of placing the order to receipt of the package at my doorstep. I then logged into CashApp and split the $450 up into the purchase of fractional shares directly from my cell phone.

The breakdown of my online purchase:

1. What kind of computer am I using? Dell
2. What is the operating system? Microsoft Windows 10
3. Who is my Internet Service Provider? AT&T
4. Where am I shopping? Amazon
5. Who makes what I wanted to buy? Apple
6. How would I pay for it? Paypal
7. Who will ship it? UPS? FedEx? Amazon?
8. Who provides the fuel? BP? Chevron? Exxon?

Using the questions above, I researched what companies were performing best in the specified industries of my breakdown.

1. HP was a cheaper stock than Dell (no serious rhyme or reason; less money spent)
2. Microsoft was stable and paying dividends
3. AT&T was stable and paying dividends
4. Amazon was a hot stock due to a spike in online shopping
5. Apple was a no brainer to purchase because they are profitable and pay dividends
6. Square was the best performing merchant stock at the time. I bought both Square and PayPal
7. UPS was spiking due to online shopping
8. Chevron was a great stock to buy in the fuel niche

This is not advice on how to go about investing. It is only a point of view on how money that was going to be spent to purchase a liability was used to invest in assets and bring a return.

Notice that there were six different industries with a leader in each. The amount applied to any single entity is not disclosed, but the $450 was spread across all six industries.

Money was actively invested using technology that has made the process very simple. I invested $450. Over the course of 30 - 40 days, my money earned $82.37, which is indeed better than the return on $5000 in a bank product.

There is no secret ingredient to share when it comes to investing in the market. Be as knowledgeable as you can about industries, companies, and products if you choose this route of investing.

Familiarize yourself with the upcoming investment types. They can be passive or active and can be a good place to start.

ETFs/Index Funds/REITs/Mutual Funds

ETFs (Exchange Traded Funds)

An exchange-traded fund, or **ETF**, is a fund that can be traded on an exchange; and like a stock, can be bought and sold throughout the day.

The previous section illustrated a creative way to decide on what stocks you can *actively* invest in. ETFs offer a *passive* entry into investing. They can be purchased fractionally as well.

Key Points about ETFs

1. **Passive management** - You don't have to manage one stock at a time, which can be expensive due to fees
2. **Low cost to acquire** – less overhead to manage makes costs competitive.
3. **Easily bought and sold** – can be transacted with apps or brokerage accounts
4. **Diversification** - a share or unit of an ETF is investing in a portfolio that holds a number of different stocks or other investments. There isn't the risk of losing one stock.
5. **Information is accessible**: easy to know what the share holds and easy to follow changes if made.

Vanguard (VOO) and SPDR (SPY) are companies that passively manage portfolios.

The S&P 500 index gives exposure to the top 500 companies in the stock market. Choose ETFs that track the S&P 500.

Index Funds

An index fund is a mutual fund whose portfolio matches a stock index. Investing in an index fund is like owning a little bit of every stock in that index. This increases exposure to the market.

Market Exposure:

Dow Jones Industrial Average - tracks 30 of the largest publicly traded firms

Dow Jones Wilshire 5000 - tracks all USA based publicly traded companies

S&P 500 - tracks 500 Large-Cap corporations

AMEX Composite - tracks all the stocks on the American Stock Exchange

NYSE Composite - tracks all common stocks on the New York Stock Exchange

Russell 3000 - tracks the largest 3000 U.S. companies

Pros: passive; never performs worse than the market; low fees due to low overhead management

Cons: never out-performs the market; not professionally managed; index determines which stocks to buy

REITs (Real Estate Investment Trusts)

A REIT is a type of real estate company that resembles a mutual fund, a stock, and a bond. It provides those lacking the expertise, time, or financial means the opportunity to invest in real estate.

These companies invest in land, apartments, hotels, office space, retail space, industrial space, mortgages, and mortgage-backed securities.

REITs have several advantages for investors:

Income. REITs provide excellent income in the form of dividends. REITs pay approximately $30 billion in dividends each year.

Liquidity. Most REITs are easily bought and sold on major stock exchanges.

Diversification. REITs invest in properties in all 50 states. REITs also don't mimic the major stock indices. They are an excellent hedge against a poorly performing stock exchange.

Equity Returns. REITs provide equity returns that beat all the major market indexes over the last 25+ years.

Tax advantages and high yields are two additional advantages of REITs.

Types of REITs

- **Equity** – revenue driven by rent and property sales
- **Mortgage** - revenue from investing in mortgages and related securities
- **Hybrid** – a combination of equity and mortgage products

Mutual Funds

Equity Funds (Stock): Long-term growth

Global: Invest around the world, which could include your own country
International: Invest in countries outside of your own
Large-Cap: Companies with over $10 billion worth of total stock value
Mid-Cap: Companies between $2 billion and $10 billion worth of total stock value
Small-Cap: Companies with less than $2 billion worth of total stock value
Sector Funds: Target certain markets, such as technology, health, financial, and more
Index Funds: Seek to mirror a specific index, such as the NASDAQ or the NYSE

Fixed Income Funds (Bond)
- focus on purchasing government and corporate debt wide variety of bond funds, with different risk levels
- "Junk bonds" have a much higher level of risk than a fund that invests primarily in government bonds; should provide a much higher return.

Money Market Funds
- funds only invest in short-term debt, like Treasury bills.
- alternative to a conventional savings account

Balanced Funds

- balanced funds invest in both stocks and debt instruments.

Cryptocurrency

This will not be an in-depth look into digital currency. While some have experienced significant gains, growth, and profits, the world of crypto is proving to be extremely vast, leaving no experts on its path. The digital currency phenomenon, however, has been declared by some to be the greatest wealth transfer of our generation. Blockchain technology is worldwide. Sitting on the sidelines could prove costly if the opportunity to participate is neglected.

Crypto investing is the exchange of dollars for tokens or coins. See the increase in value of a few currencies over a few years.

Cryptocurrencies		
	2017	2021
Bitcoin (BTC)	$3,500	$60,000
Ethereum (ETH)	$350	$4,400
Litecoin	$50	$195

Total number of cryptocurrencies in 2017: **1531**
Total number of cryptocurrencies in 2021: **13,000+**

The value of each coin above has increased considerably over three years. However, there are alternative coins that carry real opportunities for profitable gains and APY returns.

Cryyptocurrencies w/Returns: Oct '21			
	Platform	Price	APY
*USDC	Block Fi	$1.00	8.25%
*DAI	Block Fi	$1.00	8.25%
Algorand (ALGO)	Coinbase	1.85	4%
Tezos (XTZ)	Coinbase	6.65	4.63%
Cosmos (ATOM)	Coinbase	39.17	5%

While only a minute number of cryptocurrencies are mentioned here, it's important to know that coins serve purposes and solve problems. Study coins to learn about what they represent. If the functionality lines up with your belief system, that's a starting point to looking further into that coin as an asset to hold.

Listed below are the functions of the coins in the illustration on the previous page.

USDC: a great option for traditional investors looking for a low-beta investment that can generate returns better than CDs

DAI: a stable coin cryptocurrency that aims to keep its value as close to one United States dollar (USD)

Algorand (ALGO): to solve the trilemma of security, scalability, and decentralization

Tezos (XTZ): provides safety and code correctness; Tezos addresses opposition to blockchain adoption

Cosmos (ATOM): enables blockchains to transfer value with each other through IBC and Peg-Zones, while letting them maintain their self-governing state.

Research to become educated about coins before purchasing.

Do not be driven to buy coins because of **FOMO** (FEAR OF MISSING OUT)!

Common Myths About Cryptocurrencies

As with any other fringe product or service, there are many myths surrounding cryptocurrencies. *Cryptocurrencies aren't just for computer geeks and drug dealers trying to avoid the government.* Relieving yourself of these myths will permit the formulation of a more accurate opinion. It's easier to make informed decisions when your knowledge is sound.

Myths regarding cryptocurrencies:

1. **Cryptocurrency is illegal.** It depends on the country. It's legal in the United States, but there are other countries, such as Russia, that have deemed it illegal. It's unlikely the legal status will change anytime soon in the United States. It may become regulated, however.

2. **Bitcoin is the only relevant cryptocurrency.** There are thousands of other cryptocurrencies. All have their strengths and weaknesses. Bitcoin, released in 2009, is the oldest and most well-known of them. Most of the other cryptocurrencies are less than three or four years old.

Other coins, just to name a few:

Cryptocurrencies Oct '21	
Coin / Token	Price
Compound (COMP)	$353.79
Polygon (MATIC)	$1.92
Cardano (ADA)	$2.02
Shiba Inu (SHIB)	1.85
Doge (DOGE)	$0.26
SKALE (SKL)	$0.38

3. **Only criminals have a use for cryptocurrencies.** While cryptocurrencies continue to be used for illegal activity, cash is still king for illegal transactions. *Some reputable retailers accept cryptocurrencies, including Microsoft and Dell.*

4. **I can get rich quickly with cryptocurrency.** The potential for profits does exist. People have gotten wealthy through increases in the value of cryptocurrencies. However, just as many people have lost a tremendous amount of money, too. It could happen. Nothing is guaranteed.

5. **Cryptocurrencies are fiat currencies.** Most of them are. That's true. But so are the Euro and the US Dollar. *All major world currencies have abandoned a gold standard.* The US decoupled the value of gold and the US Dollar in 1933. The value of all fiat currency is based on the willingness of the public to agree that it possesses value.

6. **The government can shut down cryptocurrencies.** The government could make cryptocurrencies illegal, but shutting down the system would be next to impossible. There's no central server or location that houses a cryptocurrency system. The information is stored on the computers of every user.

    - Unless the government can find a way to shut down the internet, it would be challenging to put an end to cryptocurrencies.

7. **It's easy to mine cryptocurrencies and make money.** Entire companies have been built for the sole purpose of mining cryptocurrencies. It requires a tremendous amount of computer hardware and electricity to be successful. Unless you have several hundreds of thousands of dollars, you can't

even begin to compete. *Virtual mining options do exist.*

8. **Cryptocurrencies are subject to hacking.** Bitcoin merchants and wallets have been subject to hacking activities. However, Bitcoin itself has never been hacked. Other cryptocurrencies have similar security profiles. Insufficient security is always a potential problem with cryptocurrencies and cash. *Protect your wallet and you should be fine.*

9. **It's impossible to trace cryptocurrency transactions.** It's not easy, but it can be done. Regarding Bitcoin, the blockchain ledger lists all the transactions that have ever occurred with Bitcoins. The challenging part is linking the wallet address with the owner.

    - With enough time and effort, the government can eventually track you down. The government has seized and auctioned off millions of dollars worth of Bitcoins.

It's easy to be led astray. Cryptocurrencies are not particularly common in society, and myths are easily formed and spread.

States, countries, businesses, and even banks are buying cryptocurrencies! It is not a fluke.

Preparing to Invest in Cryptocurrency

1. Don't invest what you can't afford to lose
2. Understand what you are investing in
3. Be aware of volatility (volatility can be profitable)
4. Know your position (looking to hold or looking to sell)
5. The past does not predict the future

How to Buy Cryptocurrency

1. **Acquire a wallet** (accounts can be created on exchanges or apps)
2. **Connect your purchasing source** (bank account/credit card)
3. **Secure your wallet** (Safely store all passwords and keys for security and long-term access)

Power Plays in Cryptocurrency

Staking: earn passively while holding cryptocurrencies

Real Estate: acquire crypto-backed properties

NFTs (Non-Fungible Tokens): An **NFT** is a unit of data stored on a digital ledger, called a blockchain, which can be sold and traded.

Personal Banking Systems: finance your own projects with crypto loans

Cryptocurrencies might just be the wave of the future. They're certainly becoming more popular each year.

9 Golden Rules of Investing

Your investments are serious business. *Your financial well-being, business ventures, and retirement are largely dependent on your ability to invest your money effectively.*

The golden rules of investing will serve to elevate your thinking when it comes to your investing practices.

Consider these guidelines before you make another investment:

1. **Know your starting point.** What's your net worth? Before starting any race, you have to know where the starting line is located.

    - Take regular measurements of your financial situation to gauge your progress.

2. **Avoid investing in a business or financial instrument you aren't able to understand.** Warren Buffet has made it a point to never invest in high-tech companies for the same reason. If you lack an understanding of derivative products, that would be a good reason to stay away from investing in them.

    - If you're unclear about the fundamentals of an investment, how will you know if it's a good investment or if and when you should sell it?

3. **Try not to invest and forget.** Most investments require regular monitoring and assessment. Market conditions can change, so try to remember to check on all your investments.

    - The company whose stock you purchased might suddenly start taking on a lot of debt.

- Stay on top of the latest news and make any necessary adjustments to your investments.

4. **Look past the price and the past returns.** The real value of an investment isn't always evident by looking at the price or past performance. Take the time to dig in and see if an investment has real value.

    - Sometimes an investment is underpriced because it's a great buy.
    - Sometimes it's underpriced because it's junk.

5. **Remember to consider inflation.** Most investors forget to consider the effects of inflation when choosing investments. Investing is looking toward the future, so inflation is an important consideration.

6. **Always have the insurance coverage you need.** Few things can disrupt your finances and ability to invest more profoundly than an unforeseen disaster.

    - Whether it's a medical emergency, a tornado, or someone suing you because they slipped on your sidewalk, you want to have adequate insurance coverage to take care of it.

Make tax planning an ongoing process. Most people only plan for taxes at tax time. However, the wise investor considers tax issues throughout the entire year.

- Whenever you make an investment, consider what the tax implications might be.

- A little bit of forethought can mean thousands of dollars in April and you can beat the taxman at his own game.

7. **Have preparations in place for financial emergencies.** If you lost your job tomorrow, how long could you last financially? Would you be forced to sell your portfolio and start over? If you lack an emergency fund, consider starting one as soon as possible. When you need it, you'll be grateful that you have it.

8. **Retirement savings should take precedence.** When retirement savings isn't a priority, you usually won't have much of a retirement fund. We're all prone to putting things off until tomorrow. Start preparing for your retirement today.

- Make your retirement a priority and you'll live comfortably in your golden years.

Investing doesn't have to be complex, but it does require discipline and planning. These rules serve as a framework that will allow you to stay on track.

The take-away from this step is to learn as many ways as you can to keep your money or have it come back to you.

Nugget: I totaled up all the money that I've spent on cars over the last 10 years. If I had *invested ($100)* in legitimizing my business with the state ten years ago, I could have then leased my cars, and 100% of the payments and other auto-related expenses (money that most of us spend anyway) would have come back to me in the form of tax minimization. Consult with a tax professional to help position yourself or your children to monetize in this fashion.

STEP 6: GET INSURED

Do You Have All the Insurance You Need?

Part of your financial plan should include protecting your assets, including your possessions, as well as your income, loved ones, and health-related financial concerns. Insurance isn't very exciting, and it can certainly be expensive. But when you need it, you'll be glad you have it. Unfortunately, there's no single policy that will give you all the coverage you need.

Take inventory of your insurance coverage. Do you have these 5 important policies?

Life Insurance

Life insurance protects those who depend on you financially if you die unexpectedly. Consider the hardships on your loved ones in the event of your passing away.

Comedian George Wallace made a joke about "things people say". "He died an untimely death." was a comment that made the list. "Well when is a good time to die?" was the joke's punchline. As I shared in the early chapters, I experienced the untimely death of my father. It was a devastating loss. Fortunately, he made insurance provisions to the extent that he could for our household. Why was there an extent to which he could? When my dad was in his early twenties, he received a medical diagnosis while in the military that made him essentially uninsurable. So my message, particularly to younger readers and especially young parents is to get life insurance while the rates are affordable; and before the woes of health take a position in your life.

How do you determine how much life insurance you should get?

Consider these matters:

- Funeral expenses
- Replacing your income and for how long
- Education costs
- Existing mortgage balance

No one likes to think about these things. However, if you deal with it now, it's something your family doesn't have to deal with in addition to heartbreak. Life insurance has living benefits as well. Consult a licensed insurance producer (wink-wink) on how to build your family banking system.

Types of Life Insurance

Because people have different needs and different life situations, there are different types of life insurance to fit those needs. The majority of life insurance policies are term life, whole life, universal life, variable life, and survivorship life insurance. To determine which type would be best for you, read on.

Term Life Insurance

Term life insurance is the most basic and low-cost choice for life insurance. You simply pay a particular amount for a specific number of years. Normally, you can obtain term life insurance for 10, 15, 25, or 30-year terms.

1. The simple terms. Should you die while the policy is in force, whomever you designated as your beneficiary would receive the proceeds. However, if you come to the end of your term while living, you've completed that insurance policy and must purchase and begin paying another term of life insurance.

   1. Bear in mind that your premiums will increase along with your age. To clarify, the older you get, the more your insurance premiums will cost.

2. Guaranteed Renewal Term Life. On the other hand, you might inquire as to whether a term life insurance policy you're considering has "guaranteed renewal." Guaranteed renewal means that near the end of the term, you can go ahead and extend the policy with no worry of having to get a medical exam.

   2. Although this feature may not be all that important while you're young, it is advisable to purchase term life insurance that has guaranteed renewal.

   3. With guaranteed renewal, even if you become critically ill, you can still renew your policy without having a new medical exam to qualify for new insurance.

3. Convertible Term Life. Another aspect of term life insurance to be aware of is policy "convertibility." Many term life insurance policies allow you to "convert" the policy into a policy that has cash value, also without a physical exam.

   1. Having a cash value life insurance policy can come in handy if you should ever need to borrow money against the policy.

4. Return of Premium Term Life. You might like to choose a term life policy that pays you back if you do not die during the term. With this type, if you pay the entire life insurance term and survive, you can have returned to you, tax-free, all the money you paid in for the policy over the years.

    Rates for return of premium policies will cost you about 1-1/2 times what a "regular" term life insurance policy will. However, if you survive the term, all your money comes back to you. It's something to consider.

Reasons to Get Term Life Insurance

If you're already stretching your dollars, term life insurance tends to be the least expensive. Plus, it's the simplest form of insurance, which makes it no-fuss. Finally, you have some choices to make within the range of term life insurance vehicles, which allows you to tailor the policy to your needs (length of the term, convertibility, and return of premiums).

Whole Life Insurance

Whole life insurance has a savings aspect to it that term life insurance doesn't. With whole life insurance, the premiums you pay stay the same year after year and the policy builds cash value over time.

- How it builds cash value. Each month that you pay your monthly whole life insurance premium, part of your premium covers the actual cost of insuring your risk and the other part goes into an investment vehicle. Depending on the policy, the investment portion might go toward stocks, bonds, or a money market.

- Insurance plus tax-free growth. Whole life insurance policies provide a vehicle to invest dollars regularly while the cash value grows tax-free.

1. However, if you simply want to make an investment, doing so as a part of a whole life insurance policy usually isn't the most cost-effective type of investment.

2. A popular choice is buying term life insurance for insurance and separate investments for growing your money.

3. Your tax accountant, financial planner, or insurance agent will be able to help you choose which type of vehicle is best for your situation.

- You can borrow your cash value. With whole life, you have the choice to borrow against the cash value of the investment component, which may come in handy if you need funds for a major purchase like a home.

Reasons to Get Whole Life Insurance

In theory, if you want term life insurance plus a small investment to build over time without thinking about it, consider purchasing whole life insurance.

Plus, whole life insurance provides you with the possibility of borrowing against the accumulated value, in the event you need funds in an emergency. Whole life might be the right choice for your life insurance if these issues are important.

Universal Life

Universal life insurance has some similarities to whole life insurance. Both types of these insurances provide life insurance plus an investment vehicle that you regularly pay into.

However, universal life gives you a wider choice in your premiums and investment options, but the actual death benefit may also change according to the performance of the investments. It may go up or down.

Other items unique to universal life insurance policies are:

- Using your cash value. Like whole life, you can borrow against the cash value of your universal life insurance policy. However, unlike whole life, you can also use the cash that has built over time to pay your monthly premium. But if you use your cash value to pay your premiums for the policy, the investment value will reduce accordingly as you use it.

- Variable rates on your investment portion. The investment funds that build up over time do so at a variable rate that can change from month to month.

- The investment passes on to your beneficiary tax-free. An important aspect of universal life insurance policies is that, if left untouched, the investment portion of your premium dollars passes on, tax-free, to your beneficiaries upon your death.

Reasons to Get Universal Life Insurance

If you want the most flexibility that you can get from your life insurance policy, term life plus investment value plus the ability to pay your premiums with accumulated premium dollars, then universal life insurance is the choice for you.

Variable Life Insurance

Most of your premium dollars for variable life insurance are applied toward the investment component of the insurance. This type of policy focuses largely on the investment aspect.

1. Large choice of investments. You can select the type of investments you want to make with this type of insurance – money market, stocks, bonds, and mutual funds, to name a few. This type of life insurance behaves more like an investment account, with fund managers to manage your investments so they will hopefully build the cash you seek.

2. If your investments perform well, your death benefit will be paid off at a hefty rate. If the investment funds aren't good performers, the amount paid to your beneficiary will be lessened.

3. Variable death benefit. So, although a guaranteed amount will be paid out at the time of your death, with variable life insurance, that benefit amount will vary.

4. You can also take out a loan against your variable life insurance. The amount you're able to borrow largely depends on the type of investments you have at the time of your loan application.

Reasons to Get Variable Life Insurance

For those who are well versed in watching the stock market, a variable life insurance policy may be just the vehicle to provide you with a guaranteed payout to your beneficiary with the chance of earning a lot of extra tax-deferred or tax-free dollars. You have the opportunity to make some real cash on a variable life insurance policy.

Survivorship Life Insurance

If you anticipate accumulating over 1.3 million dollars in your lifetime (more likely than you may think), having a survivorship life insurance policy to cover both you and your spouse will prevent your heirs from having to pay estate taxes upwards of 55% of the money they inherit from you.

Survivorship life insurance, or a "second-to-die life insurance policy," pays out whenever the 2nd (last-surviving) spouse dies.

Here's how survivorship life insurance works:
As a couple, you and your spouse set up a life insurance trust to buy a life insurance policy that will pay your beneficiaries after both of you die. Consulting an estate tax attorney will give you the answers you need to set up a trust to take the best advantage of

this type of insurance.

- Your heirs can then use the policy proceeds to make up for the loss of money due to the payment of estate taxes.

- Because the policy proceeds aren't paid out until you and your spouse both die, the price of survivorship life insurance policies tend to be less than other policies.

A benefit of survivorship life insurance policies is that it doesn't matter who dies first. As long as both of your wills individually leave all the assets to the other person, you're all set. Then, upon the death of the last surviving spouse, the trust that's been paying the policy will pay your beneficiary to offset estate tax costs.

Reasons to Get Survivorship Life Insurance

If you plan to accumulate over 1 million dollars, it makes excellent sense to get a survivorship life insurance policy. Such policies prevent your heirs from losing up to half of your estate to the federal government.

Also, if you plan to leave money for charitable purposes, this type of insurance ensures there will be enough of your money left to do so through the trust you established.

A third reason to get survivorship life insurance is if you have a special needs child that will survive you and will need to be taken care of. The trust you establish for this type of insurance will be used as the vehicle for guaranteed dollars to be used to take care of your surviving special needs heir.

Reviewing the various types of life insurance helps determine which type will best meet your family's needs. Once you find an insurance professional to assist and clarify the differences, you'll be on your way to protect your family in the event of your passing away.

Health Insurance

Health insurance is expensive, but health care is expensive too, really expensive. A simple trip to the doctor can easily be several hundred dollars. A routine surgery that only results in being in the hospital for a couple of hours can be over $10,000.

Health insurance costs are a burden, but the cost of a genuine medical issue can be catastrophic. I have had hospital stays. Premiums were a drop in the buck compared to the total cost of care.

If this isn't something you can get through your employer, be prepared to do some legwork to find a policy that's right for you.

It is undeniable that health insurance makes healthcare more accessible, including preventive services such as screenings and regular check-ups with your doctor.

Consider the fact that only a third of the uninsured U.S population scheduled a preventive visit with their doctor in past years. On the other hand, 74% of adults with health insurance saw their doctor for a preventive visit during the same year.

If you don't have insurance or have a policy that doesn't meet your needs, you must learn more about healthcare coverage to find a policy that matches your needs and your budget.

Ask yourself these important questions before purchasing a policy:

1. **What is the Affordable Healthcare Act?** The purpose of the Affordable Healthcare Act is to make health insurance more accessible by extending Medicaid coverage, creating a marketplace where you can shop for policies, and requiring insurance providers to offer coverage to clients despite pre-existing health conditions.

    - *However, this law also makes it mandatory to purchase healthcare.* If you're not insured, the government no longer levies a fine with your income taxes. The mandate is not enforced at the federal level. But a handful of states still choose to set a level of compliance.

2. **Are you eligible for Medicaid or Medicare?** You're eligible for Medicare if you're over the age of 65 and have been paying Medicare tax for at least 10 years. Medicaid coverage is available on a state level, which means requirements vary depending on where you live.

    - The Affordable Care Act sets the minimum income that makes you eligible for Medicaid at 133% of the federal poverty level. It's possible that your state offers coverage to individuals who earn more.

- *Even if you're eligible for Medicaid or Medicare, you can also purchase additional coverage if you feel that these programs do not entirely meet your needs.*

3. **What are your options if you don't qualify for Medicaid or Medicare?** You still have many options:

    - You can purchase insurance on the Healthcare.gov website and possibly qualify for other subsidies.

    - You might also receive coverage through your employer.

    - If you're under the age of 24, your parents can include you on their policy.

    - In addition, you can also find alternative personal policies outside these realms.

4. **What factors should you consider when choosing a policy?** It's important to select a health insurance policy that corresponds to your needs and budget. *Consider these factors before purchasing coverage:*

    - **Monthly premiums.** This corresponds to the amount you will have to pay on a monthly basis to receive coverage.

    - **Deductible.** *This is your portion of your medical expenses – before your insurance even starts to cover your expenses.* Most policies include a co-pay for doctor appointments and a larger deductible if you need surgery or another expensive form of treatment.

- **Amount of coverage offered.** What percentage of your medical expenses will the insurance company pay? Is there a maximum amount?

- **Reputation of your health insurance provider.** Choose a company with good reviews. Your insurance provider should value customer service and process claims quickly and efficiently.

5. **Which factors influence your health insurance premiums?** Your premiums are based on how likely you are to need coverage for medical expenses. *These are the factors healthcare insurance providers look at:*

   - **Your age.** Purchasing healthcare coverage while you're young and healthy will help you secure low premiums.

   - **Your location.** The cost of living in your area can affect your premiums.

Smoking. Using tobacco could result in your premiums being 50% higher than the premiums offered to a non-smoker.

   - **The type of plan you purchase.** *Premiums are higher for policies with lower out-of-pocket amounts.*

There are many downsides to not having healthcare, including putting off screenings for some health conditions and not scheduling regular check-ups with your doctor. Should you become ill or injured, you would end up with huge medical bills.

A more important question to ask yourself might be, "Can I afford *not* to have health insurance?"

Long-Term Disability Insurance

This insurance replaces a portion of your lost income if you become unable to work. The cost depends on the amount of income that you wish to replace, your age, health, the length, and the limits of coverage. Policies will also differ regarding what they consider to be a "disability."
This coverage can also be quite expensive. Hopefully, you can also get this through your employer. If not, sit down with your life or health insurance agent to go over the details of this important insurance.

Most of us have insured our house, possessions, cars, and our lives. However, **have you insured something that might be even more important: your ability to consistently earn income?** This may be the most important asset you have.

Consider the following: if you currently earn $50,000 a year and you're 35 years old, from now until you're 65 you'll earn $1.5 million. That assumes your income never increases, which it almost certainly will.

Doesn't that seem like it might be worth protecting? Is your house or car worth $1.5 million? Most of us don't own any single object worth $1.5 million.

What Are the Chances of Actually Needing to Use Your Disability Insurance?

Disability insurance insures your ability to earn income. Many people hear the word "disability" and immediately think of an accident. But most long-term disabilities are the result of illness, such as heart disease or cancer. **Every year, over 12% of adults in the United States have a long-term disability.**

Not only that, but one out of seven employed residents of the United States will have a disability that lasts 5 years or longer before age 65. *The odds of suffering a disability that lasts at least 3 months is over 50 percent.* And the U.S. Department of Housing and Urban Development has estimated that 45 percent of foreclosures are due to disability.

What about social security? Social security does provide benefits, but qualifying is not always easy. The benefits provided are rather limited, even for the most frugal of people.

How to Get Disability Insurance

Large employers typically offer short-term and long-term disability insurance. This coverage is frequently affordable and will cover 50-60% of your salary. The total payout may also be capped.

If you prefer or need to go with an individual policy instead of through your employer, be aware that they can be quite expensive, but have far more flexibility to provide what you need. The cost of an individual policy can vary dramatically, but expect to annually pay 1%-3% of your salary to replace 60% of your salary.

Some factors that influence the premium include:
1. **The monthly payout.** Obviously, the more money you would receive in the event you suffer a disability, the more your policy will cost.

2. **How "disability" is defined.** Does it pay if you are unable to do your job? Or does it only pay if you are unable to do your job and any other job for which you're qualified? What if you can work part of a day, but not the whole day? *Be sure you*

know what you're getting, and what you're not getting.

3. **How long is the waiting period before you start receiving your payments?** The longer the waiting period, the less expensive the policy will be.

    - This is a good reason to have that 4-6 month cash reserve you're always hearing about. If you don't currently have it set aside, get started today!

4. **Your occupation.** Some jobs are simply more hazardous than others. Everything else being equal, a construction worker should expect to pay more than an accountant.

5. **Cost of living.** Some policies cover the cost of living increases. This can make a big difference, depending on the length of your disability.

6. **Additional purchase option.** Once you're insured, this option would allow you to purchase additional coverage later on without having to submit to another physical exam.

Disability insurance is the insurance that everyone seems to forget about, especially those who are self-employed. But this may be the most important insurance you can purchase! Look into disability insurance today; your future and the future of your family may depend on it.

Homeowner's Insurance

If you still owe money on your home, your lender requires homeowner's insurance. If you don't owe money on your home, you should still carry this type of financial protection. Consider how many thousands of dollars your house and the contents would cost to replace.

The price of homeowners insurance is quite small compared to the amount of coverage you're getting.

Besides covering the structure of the house and its contents, some policies will even cover putting you up in a hotel until your house is repaired. Any injuries that occur to friends and strangers are also covered under your house policy.

Consider what you need; there are a lot of options for benefits, limits, and price.

Automobile Insurance

Nearly all states require automobile insurance to varying degrees (New Hampshire is the exception). Everyone should have coverage, even if you drive a 1975 Chevy Nova that has been paid off for years. Even in that case, you're still financially responsible for the damage you cause to other vehicles and property.

Without automobile insurance, you might face a lawsuit that could potentially cost you everything you own. Ensure you have all the coverage you need, not only for your own vehicle but to cover your liability as well.

I conclude by saying that we are all 1 accident, 1 hospital stay, or 1 liable occurrence away from what could cause financial disaster for our households and loved ones. As it relates to personal finance, the low costs of premiums in exchange for thousands of dollars of coverage are an intelligent way to protect your personal finances. In the absence of policies in these areas, you are otherwise considered "self-insured"; and you will carry the financial responsibility of any incidents as an individual.

Insurance isn't exciting or sexy, but it's a necessity. When looking at new policies, shop around because prices and coverage can differ widely from one company to the next.

One tip to save some money: Get a policy with a higher deductible. The more you have to pay before the insurance kicks in, the less that insurance coverage will cost you.

Do your homework and find an insurance professional you can trust. Don't just focus on what insurance costs you; think of what it will cost you if you don't have it.

STEP 7: BOOST YOUR SKILLS

Increase Your Earning Potential Without Loans

I've met young people who were hired by companies to serve in an array of different capacities. It was largely because they carried highly demanded skillsets like graphic design, computer programming, and web content development to name a few.

Ironically they were all self-educated, having used tools and resources that today's technology makes available. I can attest to alternative methods of becoming educated and acquiring a skillset. I completed self-study courses and computer-based training programs during my acquisition of IT certifications.

Quality learning and education are no longer limited to the traditional routes of years ago. One of the greatest benefits of the current information age is that it has leveled the playing field between those who know and those who need to know. Just as the printing press helped to widen literacy beyond the clergy or ruling class in the 15th century, so too has the Internet widened access on almost every topic to anyone with a computer in the 21st century.

Not too long ago, anyone who wanted to gain a high degree of knowledge and skills had to attend college. *Today, exceptional online resources and a better appreciation of learning through experience have widened the learning forum.*

Some of the high-demand professions today require skills that can be developed through independent study using online resources, internships, and mentorships.

Interactive and professionally developed seminars and conferences are available on almost every career specialty.

The distinctive attribute of independent learning resources today is that they are multi-faceted. The tools and services that you can access online, in your community, or across the country are more varied to suit the needs and preferences of the 21St-century learner.

There are tools and resources for learning today that make it easy to see the potential for reaching your educational goals without following the long, costly, and sometimes irrelevant college route.

Attending college is only one educational option. Depending on your professional needs and life priorities, there may be far more effective and beneficial alternatives to achieving your educational goals.

Here are some of the tools that offer comprehensive, recognized, and effective learning opportunities:

- *Audio files* that can deliver hours of content to you while you drive or in my case, for example, shower. I've learned several financial strategies by choosing to listen to subject matter experts versus music on the radio in my car.

- *Videos* that allow you to watch an instructor deliver demonstrations. YouTube is filled with educational content. Khan academy is awesome.

- *Live, interactive online seminars and conferences* where you can participate in person or online

- Professional associations and peer groups offering **one-on-one mentorship and coaching** to guide learners through programs and the newest practices in their field

- **Internships** sponsored by large employers and small business owners that want experienced people and are willing to educate eager learners through onsite opportunities

Find ways to leverage the following resources to boost your skills and increase your ability to earn.

Library

I've visited libraries for different reasons (not as much in pandemic times) and I am always intrigued as to why they remain heavily populated. It's not complicated, I suppose. The local library is a bank of **free** information and **free** technology. Citizens can attend workshops and seminars free of charge, which adds value to the presence of these facilities.

1. **Current periodicals (magazines, regularly published journals, newspapers).** If you were to subscribe to these, they could cost you hundreds or thousands of dollars in subscription fees. Yet, at the library, they're free for you to use.

    - Some of the professional periodicals – for instance, internationally acclaimed magazines for meeting planners, graphic designers, writers, or life coaches – offer some of the best and most current information on best practices, new procedures, and business management models.

- As a member of your local library, you can in many cases sign out these materials to use at home or obtain access to these publications online. Check with your local librarian for details.

2. **Books in your field.** As you delve into the topic of your choice, you'll surely find great books that offer excellent information. Fulfilling your potential book list could cost you hundreds of dollars if you didn't have the library.

    - Not every book on your booklist will be one that you'll want to keep, so why not sign it out, make notes of relevant information, and return the book when you're done? That could be one less book gathering dust on your shelves.

    - *Save your book purchase money for those books and guides you know you'll be referring to again and again* or those that you simply enjoy and want as part of your permanent collection.

3. **Professional advice.** Your local library is staffed with professionals who have a wealth of knowledge about reference materials, local organizations, and services that may be of interest and relevance to your learning program.

    Bring your queries and concerns about resources, topics, and learning options to your librarian. If your library is well-staffed, you'll end up saving yourself hours of searching and you may even pick up a few good short-cuts as well!

4. **A varied learning environment.** Even though you may be choosing to educate yourself independently, that doesn't mean that you should keep yourself sequestered in your

home. Your tax dollars pay for your local, cozy library – so enjoy it! The idea is to stay relevant!

Internet

The internet offers opportunity and information access that was once only available to institutions and entities with significant resources.

The internet levels the playing field regarding access to knowledge because it's:

- Affordable
- Available to anyone with a computer
- Constantly evolving to reflect the needs of users in our age

Tremendous Access to Knowledge

With millions of users sharing information in forums, discussion groups, and blogs and millions of organizations making their own data available via websites, there are now databases and information on just about any topic.

For example:

- **The choice is all yours.** There are thousands of websites you can access from the comfort of your desk that contain videos, audio files, and eBooks to show you how to get started in any business you choose.

- **Multi-media access has changed the learning landscape.** The internet is multi-dimensional. Video, audio, and interactive resources like live online seminars can help you develop skills in everything from a new language to how to fix machinery.

The resources online are growing exponentially on a daily basis, so if you feel the need to get some opinions on where to start your educational journey, try using an online resource to also help narrow your search.

Connecting Users to Knowledge Groups

You can start by first locating a popular and credible online discussion group or forum on your topic. *Their discussions educate all forum participants.* A visit to a site like this can give you a variety of opinions on a particular resource or service.

For example, if you'd like to learn how to become a technical editor but aren't sure which training program to purchase or participate in, you might want to get a recommendation from a peer group at a forum for technical editors.

You can search out such a group by using search engines like Google, MSN, or Yahoo. Search "Finding a Mentor" for more information on this topic.

E-books

The introduction of e-books in recent years has empowered those in pursuit of independent learning and practical education in enormous ways.

Not only is more information now available online via e-books, but it's also affordable and responsive to the needs of users. There's no waiting for delivery or hefty shipping costs.

You simply purchase the e-book you want online and gain access to it almost immediately.

So if your schedule is such that 3:00 in the morning is your best time for searching out and reading new educational material, you can do that if the materials you require are available as e-books.

Environmentally Friendly

A great benefit of using e-books is that these resources aren't printed on paper. You can read your e-book on your computer screen and avoid the destruction of more trees.

Of course, it's wise to have an organized system of filing your e-books on your computer so you can find them when you need to. Also, be sure to back up your files using an online file backup storage service or an external hard drive.

Seminars and Conferences

Many people require face-to-face interaction with others to retain and learn topics and skills effectively. That's why educational seminars and conferences are so popular. With technology, you can attend a conference hosted in Denver while living in Atlanta! I try to attend 2 or 3 conferences per year in my niche.

For some people, the thought of reading a 300-page textbook is inconceivable! You can break it down to ten pages a day, equating to one book per month. However, some comprehensive seminars on particular topics can provide as much – if not more – practical knowledge as a densely written textbook.

In-depth learning seminars may range from a few hours in length to several days and can include in-depth discussions, presentations, and other learning activities that encourage retention and comprehension.

Whereas seminars focus on one topic, conferences often focus on a particular field or subject area.

They can include a number of related workshops where smaller groups are involved in more hands-on, interactive activities. There may also be sessions where one speaker or panel discussion group addresses all the conference attendees.

Contact a professional association or mentorship group in your field to learn about available seminars and conferences. Such groups often sponsor or produce such events and also promote related events that may interest you.

Find a Mentor

A mentor is an individual, always more experienced, who's trusted by another to help and counsel them for some purpose or cause. **Mentors are very popular in the workplace!** They help people navigate and develop their careers or businesses.

This is an enormous educational opportunity. Mentors can provide encouragement and help you avoid costly mistakes in your educational development. A mentor has experience in the work you want to do and is more often at a senior level.

Your mentor can give you information based on hands-on experience, not just theory.

Mentors can also save you a lot of time by directing you to the best resources available to help you achieve your educational and professional goals.

Where to Find a Mentor

You can find a mentor in a number of ways:

1. **Join a mentorship group for your field.** For example, if you want to become a professional speaker, it would be wise to join one of the most recognized professional speakers' associations in the region or your country.

    - Professional associations often offer mentorship opportunities, pairing up new members with more experienced members.

    - They may provide discussion groups and forums where all members can discuss issues and ask questions. Newer members can then learn from and create relationships with experienced members through participating in discussions within the forum.

2. **Attend seminars and conferences.** Take note of those presenters who've impressed you with their knowledge and experience.

    - Make an effort to make a connection with them at the event or obtain their contact information so that you can communicate your admiration for their work and interest in looking to them for mentorship advice.

3. **Conduct online research to identify leaders in your field.** Try to locate local leaders so that you'll have an opportunity to have more face-to-face opportunities to meet with your mentor.

Become an Intern

One of the best ways to get an education about a particular job or career is to get an intern position.

An internship is a work arrangement whereby the "intern" works in a temporary position with an emphasis on on-the-job training rather than necessarily securing employment. ***Internships can be paid or unpaid.***

The benefit of an internship is that you get hands-on experience in the field of your interest. For some learners, practical experience is far more effective than theoretical learning through books alone.

Another benefit of an internship is that potential employers look favorably upon candidates that have experience in a job through internships or otherwise.

As an intern, you're not expected to know everything about your field, so you can make mistakes without losing your job. It's an ideal way to learn on the job while receiving the support and attention of those in the work environment.

Between online resources, peer group organizations, seminars, and conferences, there are viable and effective alternatives to college when searching out an education to secure your career or business goals.

Choose educational resources and methods that respond to *your* particular learning needs for the most successful learning outcome.

CONCLUSION

Fixing broke isn't just about how much money you make. All components of personal finance are relevant. They make up a holistic approach to building financial stability and prosperity.

Refer back to this list of components for your own use as well as for others you engage about personal finance.

1. **A money mindset.** A positive financial belief system will promote faith, confidence, and discipline without being limited by traditional money myths or negative thoughts.

2. **Budget.** Whether you're earning minimum wage or running the most successful hedge fund the world has ever seen, a budget is important.

   - Know how much you're spending and where the money is being spent. There's no way around it. The information is valuable to you and provides boundaries that ensure your financial success.

3. **Strategically live off less than what you make.** If your bills outpace your income, you're going to have financial woes. Everyone would be wise to increase their income and lower their bills.

4. **An emergency fund.** *Life is neither perfect nor predictable.* Sooner or later, an unexpected expense will occur. Many families are only a few weeks away from being homeless if sudden unemployment or a major expense occurs.

5. **A minimal amount of consumer debt.** No matter how much money you have or make, it's very easy to create more debt than you can handle.

    - Avoid consumer debt whenever possible. Especially avoid debt to purchase items that lose value.

6. **Controlled spending.** It's also easy to spend more than you make. Are you an impulsive shopper? Do you like to purchase items that are out of your income bracket? Do you enjoy giving your money away to retailers?

7. **Saving regularly.** Are you saving a percentage of each and every paycheck? With the regular habit of saving, anyone can retire in style. Always **PAY YOURSELF FIRST**!

8. **Investing your savings appropriately.** Saving is great, but leaving your money in a savings account is less than ideal. Do your investing activities address your needs? Are you saving for retirement? Don't be a full-time consumer! Put your money to work.

9. **The necessary insurance to prevent financial catastrophe.** A serious illness, fire, or death can derail the best-laid plans.

10. **Continued education is the key to remaining relevant.**
    - *Audio files / Videos*
    - *One-on-one mentorship and coaching*
    - *Live, interactive online seminars and conferences* where you can participate in person or virtually

As time goes on, it may become difficult to stick to your financial goals. Challenges may arise that tempt you to put your plans aside. As mentioned in the introduction, I trust that you will operate in the **Termination Stage of Behavior Change**, which is putting together the components of personal finance, working your system, and maximizing financial capabilities for yourself and your seed.

THE END

RESOURCES

For a list of resources to empower you on your personal finance journey, visit: www.efifinancial.net/resources